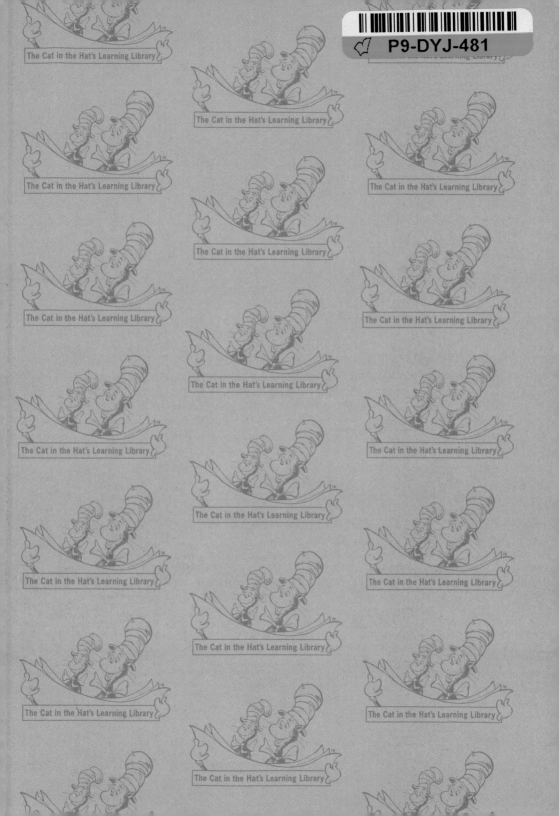

The editors would like to thank
BARBARA KIEFER, Ph.D., Associate Professor of Reading and Literature,
Teacher's College, Columbia University, and
ROBERT ASHER of the Doctoral Program in Anthropological Sciences,
State University of New York, Stony Brook,
for their assistance in the preparation of this book.

Library of Congress Cataloging-in-Publication Data
Worth, Bonnie.
Oh say can you say di-no-saur? / by Bonnie Worth.   p.   cm. —
(The Cat in the Hat's learning library)
SUMMARY: Dr. Seuss's Cat in the Hat shows Sally and Dick how dinosaur fossils
are excavated, assembled, and displayed in a museum.
ISBN 0-679-89114-5 (trade). — ISBN 0-679-99114-X (lib. bdg.)
1. Dinosaurs—Juvenile literature. [1. Dinosaurs.] I. Title. II. Series.
QE862.D5W67 1998 567.9—dc21 97-52314

Printed in the United States of America   10 9 8 7 6 5 4 3 2 1

GROLIER
B O O K S
BOOK CLUB EDITION

Oh say can you say Di-no-saur?

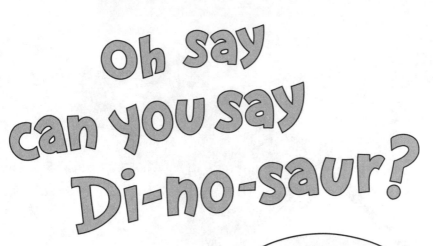

by
Bonnie
Worth

illustrated
by
Steve
Haefele

The Cat in the Hat's Learning Library™

Random House 🏠 New York

I'm the Cat in the Hat
(you have met me before).
Today I will speak
of the great dinosaur!

Dinosaurs lived
on the earth long ago,
before you and me.
So how do we know?

From fossils!
Dinosaur teeth, eggs, and bone
got stuck in the muck.
Then that muck turned to stone.

These fossils are old.
They are dusty and worn
because they were made
long before you were born.

8

Not hundreds of years,
not thousands of years,
but **millions** of years—
long before you were born!

Dinosaur hunters
dig in the ground.
All over the earth
these fossils are found.

The hunters use tools
to chip-chip all day.
The fossils come loose,
then they pack them away.

Fossils can crumble because they are old, so dinosaur hunters must first make a mold.

To the dinosaur labs
every bone, tooth, and bit
is carefully shipped
to see how they fit.

Is this a leg bone?
Maybe a muzzle?
It's a crazy,
mixed-up
dinosaur
puzzle!

Step up and enter
the Museum Hall,
where dinosaurs stand.
Some are big.
Some are small.

Here we will play
the best of all games:
Oh Say Can You Say
the Dinosaurs' Names?

16

Take care of your father,
sweet Sally, dear Dick.
These long words can make
even grownups feel sick!

And after you've said 'em,
you then get to see 'em—
in the Cat in the Hat's
Super Dino Museum.

Dinosaur names
are not easy to read.
But give it a try.
(I will help if you need.)

Oh say can you say
ANG-
kih-
luh-
saw-
rus?
With a club for a tail
and a back full of spikes,
this dino was strong—
like an army tank. Yikes!

ANKYLOSAURUS

Now can you say
MY-
uh-
saw-
ruh?
There's one thing we know
that this dino did best.
She kept her kids cozy
and safe in their nest.

She kept the nest tidy.
She got her kids food.
She was a good mother
to her dino brood.

MAIASAURA

TYRANNOSAURUS REX

Now say
tie-
RAN-
uh-
saw-
rus
rex!
You said that quite nicely—
now you'd better go.
T. rex is no kitten,
I think you should know.

This T. rex was strong,
with long teeth sharp as knives.
When most dinos saw him,
they ran for their lives!

T. rex was a hunter.
He hunted for meat.
Other dinosaurs were
his idea of a treat.

"Carnivore" is
the name that we give
to dinos like this
who ate meat to live.

TRICERATOPS

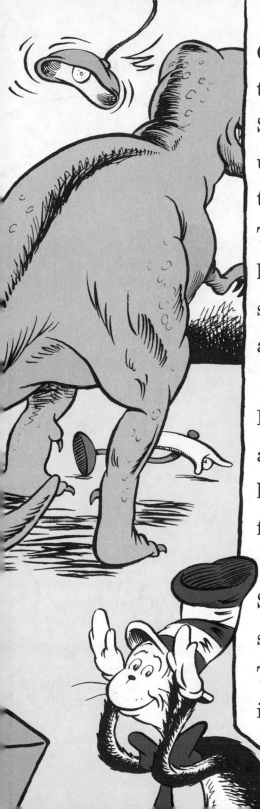

Oh say can you say
try-
SEHR-
uh-
tops?
This dinosaur's head
had three horns upon it,
sticking up out of
a hard sort of bonnet.

But though he was smaller
and not half as fierce,
his head was too hard
for T. rex teeth to pierce.

So after a few dozen
snaps at his face,
T. rex looked for dinner
in some other place.

APATOSAURUS

Oh say can you say
uh-
PAT-
uh-
saw-
rus?

I've gotten this rather tall
ladder here for us
to see eye to eye
with Apatosaurus.

These dinos' long necks
reached up high into trees,
where they fed on green leaves—
just as much as they'd please!

"Herbivore" is
the name that we give
to dinos like these
who ate plants to live.

Can you say

BRACK-

ee-

uh-

saw-

rus?

This dino was taller

than fifty-one feet!

And just how much food

do you think he could eat?

Nearly as much

as a truckload of hay

is what he would gobble,

day after day.

BRACHIOSAURUS

That's how he grew
to this size, as you see.
The Cat in the Hat
just comes up to his knee!

ZUCCHINI

BRAIN

He's nowhere as smart
as a you or a me.
His brain is the size
of a small zoo-KEY-nee!

IGUANODON

Oh say can you say

ih-

GWAN-

uh-

don?

What he did with his thumb

we think that we know.

We think that he used it

to jab at his foe.

DEINONYCHUS

Now say
die-
NON-
ih-
kus!
"Terrible claw"
is what its name means.
We think that this
dinosaur hunted in teams.

ARCHAEOPTERYX

Can you say

    are-

    key-

    OP-

    ter-

    ix?

This fine feathered friend

is the earliest known.

This bird might have glided.

This bird might have flown.

One thing we must ask,

and we must be quite firm:

If this bird was so early...

...did he catch the worm?

It's getting late now.
I see night is falling.
The Museum is closing.
Your mother is calling.

Before you head home,
dear Sally and Dick,
I have a surprise
that is really quite slick.

This dino's the earliest
cat that is known.
No one has seen it.
It's never been shown.
It's super, terrific!
It stands here before us.
Oh say can you say...

cat-
in-
the-
HAT-
uh-
saw-
rus?

CATINTHEHATOSAURUS

GLOSSARY

Brood: A number of young hatched all at one time.

Carnivore: An animal that eats flesh.

Dinosaurs: Meaning "terrible lizards," this is the name of the large group of reptiles that lived 210 million years ago. Most dinosaurs died out 65 million years ago.

Fierce: Wild, savage, and mean.

Foe: An enemy.

Fossils: The remains or the impressions of animals or plants that lived millions of years ago.

Gobble: To swallow and eat in a hurry.

Herbivore: An animal that eats plants.

Jab: To poke with something sharp.

Labs: Short for laboratories, these are the places where scientists conduct tests and experiments to find the answers to many questions.

Muck: Dirty, slimy, rotting plant and animal matter.

Museum: A building where objects of interest or value are kept and shown.

Muzzle: The part of an animal's head that sticks out—jaws, mouth, and nose.

Pierce: To make a hole with something sharp.

Zucchini (zoo-KEY-nee)**:** A green variety of squash having a long shape. While the brain of a brachiosaur was only the size of a small zucchini, the average human brain is bigger than a grapefruit!

INDEX